# ONE
# VOICE
## FOR MANY
## *Hearts*

## AN ANTHOLOGY OF POEMS BY

### Wayne A. C. Smith

ISBN 978-976-96536-3-4

**Credits:**

**Cover Design:**
Geek Resource Centre – geekjamaica@gmail.com

**Publisher:**
The Publisher's Notebook Limited
Email: thepublishersnotebook@gmail.com

2021

# Dedication

Dedicated to the blest memories of my parents Basil & Nina,
and my little sister Sarita

# Table of Contents

# Grief & Loss



# Special Occasions



# Tribute to Essential Workers

# ONE VOICE

# FOR

# MANY HEARTS

# Preface

As a child growing up in Kingston, Jamaica I would watch my mother write poems. I always admired how she would put words together so beautifully.

I was entered into the poetry competition at Bridgeport High School's annual Eisteddfod by my Literature teacher, Miss Phillips. I was petrified because I had a speech impediment courtesy of my father, who spoke through his teeth. I was glad that the "ordeal" was over! To my horror, even though I won bronze for my recital of "The Steps" by Andrew Linton, I was chosen to perform that said piece at graduation that year. I performed it and it was well-received. Whilst attending Kingston College (high school), because I didn't "speak up", my History teacher nicknamed me "Mumbly"!

After high school, I left Jamaica for Trinidad & Tobago to study Engineering. My parents were poor and had no money to give me. I collected my student grant for boarding from the Bank of Jamaica and my god-mother Daphne sent me off with pocket money, which soon ran out! Whilst in Trinidad, my mother used to send me her own monetary currency – poetry! In her letters, she never enclosed any bank drafts (which I wished for); instead, she occasionally included poetry, expressing her love for me and encouraging me to persevere!

I returned to Jamaica and started working a few months afterwards. A year after I started working, I lost my mom. Two years later, I lost my father. And, five years later, I lost my little sister. The grief I suffered allowed me to empathize with people who lost their loved ones. I formed a habit of writing words of comfort in the form of poetry for them.

Whilst in the workplace, I sometimes had the good fortune of hosting staff functions, such as retirements, send-offs, baby showers and a graduation.  I usually wrote and read poetry for these functions. Consequently, one year, my pixie gifted me two poetry books.  When I was being expatriated to the U.S. on assignment, as parting gifts, my colleagues gave me to two poetry books and an Amazon gift card.  I put aside the poetry books and immediately focused on buying something from Amazon. (Ironically, when I arrived in the U.S., my brother read Rudyard Kipling's IF to me.  Following which, I kept it on my desk.)  It wasn't until the onset of the coronavirus pandemic in 2020, that I read the two books that my colleagues gave me in 2015.

Over the years, I've given a listening ear to family members, friends and colleagues, who've lost a loved one or faced hardships and disappointments.  Outside the workplace, I've written and read poetry at funerals and weddings.  Besides listening and helping where I can, I tried to capture what their hearts were experiencing in comforting words and shared it with them.  Over the years, I noticed a common thread: these people constantly encouraged me to publish my poetry.

In 2020, my friends grew impatient with their urgings for me to publish.  Two of them even sent me contact information for a few publishers.

**One Voice For Many Hearts** is a result of finally heeding the calls from numerous people to publish some of my pieces.

# Acknowledgments

I wish to thank my wife Michele and daughter Juliet for their encouragement to pursue this project.  I thank my family, friends and co-workers who have been prompting me for years to publish my work.

# MOTIVATION
# &
# INSPIRATION

# The Confident Flower

There once was a flower, so beautiful and bright.
It grew lovelier and prettier toward heavenly light.
One day, this flower came to the realization,
That its flowerpot was its only limitation.
"Why don't you get transplanted?"
Its deep, inner feelings chanted.
"Why don't you with us stay?"
Its best friends began to pray.

Oh, what an awful decision!
I pray for utmost precision.
Oh, I must stay in this flowerpot,
The world's garden may be too hot.
"This flowerpot is too small for you,
Didn't you realize how much you grew?"
Staying in this pot, I will remain smaller,
Going out, my roots and stems will grow taller.

"They're waiting for you to fill your space,
Take the challenge, for you are an ace."
But what if I fail?
"Oh, but you are not frail;
You are not just a flower; you are a sweet rose,
Fragrant to friends, but thorny to foes!
Now take your majestic stand
For your life is the global brand!"

# I Appreciate Me

I searched and searched, but couldn't find the
answer I wanted
I looked and looked, but couldn't see the real me
I gazed and gazed into the sky, day after day
Was it me?  Why me?  When did I get here?
How did I come to this?

After a long gaze through the window, I saw shifting
scenes:
The sun was glorious and resplendent,
But there they were cussing and fussing:
"The sun is too hot."
Here it comes, rain to water the spring flowers, but
what's that I hear:
"Go away rain, you are messing up our game."
Wow, is that snow I see, so pure, so white, so
nice...but uh-oh, they're still cussing:
"Snow is too cold, it's freezing our fingers."

So, what then? Oh, I get the point, I feel it hitting
me.
I am thinking that it was all my fault, but think with
me:
You can be as brilliant as the sun but still be
unappreciated;
You can be as precious as the rain but still be
unaccepted;
You can be as pure as the snow and still be
unwanted.

So, I walk away from the window, with a sense of
me...
I am ME...
I am gifted, talented, beautiful, sensual, wonderful,
But I am not always loved as me.
So, like the sun, I still have to shine a smile
Like the rain, I still have to shower the love
Like the snow, I still have to keep a cool head

Yes, I still have to be me...just me...
Me, Confident, magnificent, resplendent,
Me...gifted, talented, sophisticated!
Me...admirable, adorable, desirable!

# Quiet Noise

Oh no! Not again
I'm on lock-down
Mood is changing
The missing puzzle:
Why me?
Options, options...
The situation: Run or be killed!

I'm such an idiot
Did I need him that badly?
I guess he was the best of the worst
Now, I want to run from this monster
I want to run, I want to hide
I want to stand, I want to retaliate
I want to scream, I want to swear!

I'm so confused
Is dark light, is up down?
Is pain pleasure, is noise quiet?
Give me black devil over white devil
Give me death over life...please
Because this is not the life I ran to
Now the smile is plastic
But the inward tears are real
Can't hide them much longer
They'll soon cover the smiles

Don't tell me it's God
Teaching me a lesson
Why doesn't he teach

This bastard a lesson instead?
Don't quote from a holy book
I can only relate to a human touch
That can help me...or, deeply hurt me
I may as well shift the curse words
From my mind to my lips
But I'm afraid of the impact
The consequence is more suffering
Well, what the hell!

Can I end it...please?
I want to escape, I want to escape
I can't take this abuse anymore!
I want to go somewhere
Somewhere, where I can't be hurt
I want to run to someone
To help me kill the memories, momentarily
Someone who cares deeply about me
I want to fast forward to the end
To the end of this cruelty
Hey, I can see it, I can feel it
Yes, that somewhere...where I'm relieved
That space to which I've escaped!
Yeah, somehow...I'm free!

# Still Here

Unspeakable cruelty,
Gut-wrenching brutality,
Befell my dark path.
My closest were helpless.
While words on deaf ears fell,
Tears spoke volumes in darkness.
Tears alone told the tale
How men of darkness clad in light
How their darkness hurt and haunt.
No light, but long, dark tunnel
No sunrise, just bleak horizon
No silver lining, only dreary clouds.
I fell below rock bottom
Into the darkest hell
But,

**I'M STILL HERE!**

Like a vicious acid attacking a base
I'm formed - salt, savour to food.
Body brutally violated;
Mind miraculously liberated.
From the depths of wickedness,
I arise a sparkly, majestic gem.
And,

**I'M STILL HERE!**

The mem'ries...
Oh, the awful memories
Cause excruciatingly
Deep distress.
You don't believe me
So I try to keep it in,
But tears belie my attempt.
My pent-up pain "released"
In droplets from my cheeks.
Someone who sees and knows,
Bottles up my precious tears.
What's the reason I'm alive?
Heaven knows I tried to end it
But love has no end.
Yes, I'm sooooo loved.
Sooo,

**I'M STILL HERE!**

Whhhhhhyyyyyyyyyyyyyyyyy?

Butterfly springs from
Struggling caterpillar's cocoon.
Sweet fragrance ascends from the
Crushed rose.
Diamond appears from
Pressured coal.
If these negatives make positives
Then Impossible means "I'm possible."

# I'M STILL HERE

because
I am a unique species
A one-of-a-kind creature
A person perfectly pretty
A woman wonderfully strong
A belle beautifully amazing
A lady elegantly gorgeous
A princess magically majestic
A peach succulently sweet
A dame deliciously sexy
Everything combined equals me,
The classy me!

# Pura Vida

My Costa Rican friends, Ticos
Love to say "Pura Vida!":
"Everything's great" or "everything's cool."
A state of thankfulness for what they have
Not dwelling on the negative!

Life throws different things at us
At unexpected times.
But always bear in mind
Even out of chaotic situations,
There can come a beautiful design

Sometimes we're victorious and feel happy,
But sometimes we lose and feel disappointed.
Losses teach us more than wins because,
Out of losses comes a determination
Unlike any other experience can teach.
So, rise beautifully from your "ashes"!

Out of "disaster",
Can come something wonderful.
Like a photographer developing "Negatives" to
create pictures
Develop your strengths
To make your life beautiful!

# The Eagle

The eagle flies high-
Keep soaring, sometimes solo
To new heights by grit!

# Light Within

People positive...
Sparking light inside of you
Shines brightly without.

# The Mind

Believe in yourself!
Remove perceived obstacles
Creative mind freed

# Keep on Running

For all the effort that you put in,
Sure... you expected better,
But the opposite is true.
You feel under-appreciated, under-valued.
You're not getting the recognition you deserve.
But isn't it good to know that someone,
Though flawed,
Values you,
Appreciates you,
And loves you?

Keep on running
Outlast the field of those
Who don't see your true worth.
Leap over obstacles!
It may not be a physical barrier.
It could be a subconscious barrier
Erected inside you.
So, tear it down or leap over it.

And, keep on running!

# Dawn

Daybreak

But before daylight

There's darkness,

There's pain,

There's horror

But as dawn follows darkness

So too will my daylight come!

# Don't Despair

Whatever you do, do NOT despair!
That only leads you to a dark place,
from which it's hard to return.
I've been there, but thankfully I'm back!
You feel like you want to end it all!
No progress with anything...
There are options you can use
to get out of this situation.
Just trust your spirit!

It may be that what you pray for
You may NOT get.
The answer to your prayer may be "NO"!
Though disappointed, deep down, be at peace in
your spirit.
And, no matter what, remain thankful throughout

Sometimes the way forward is shown by the way
blocked,
In a painfully disappointing way!
We cry, count our losses, and try to make sense of
the signs.
Broken by many gut-wrenching situations:
A "broken" person is a powerful person!

As long as you don't spend too much time
Trying to unlock closed doors,
Your life will be less stressful.
Walk away from the closed "doors",
and go forward in victory!
Remember, "NO" is a blessing!

# Vantage Point

One person sees a mountain and says,
"This is where the journey ends."
Another sees the same mountain and says,
"Challenge accepted!"
It's all about faith's perspective.

What you see as insurmountable,
Faith sees as completely moveable.
Your faith can move your perceived mountain,
And cast it into the sea.
What troubles your heart most
Can be addressed by your faith.
Desire, believe and watch the results!

# *You*

An unplanned respite
Untimely, but wisely use
To focus on YOU!

# *Me*

A moment to breathe
Reflecting and visioning...
I see future ME!

# GRIEF & LOSS

# No Matter What

No matter how deep the sorrows...
No matter how tough the fight...
No matter how thick the shadows...
No matter how dark the night...
**His eyes light the way for you.**

No matter why you fight the tears...
No matter why you cannot smile...
No matter why you hide the fears...
No matter why you feel so vile...
**His face saddens to empathize with you.**

No matter when you hear sad news...
No matter when you want to cry...
No matter when you feel the blues...
No matter when you see a dark sky...
**His arms open to comfort you.**

No matter who brings doubt to your mind...
No matter who upsets your soul...
No matter who is being so unkind...
No matter who tries to take control...
**His feet clear the path for you.**

No matter what the devil throws...
No matter what He allows to hit you...
No matter what may be the woes...
No matter what you're going through...
**His heart loves you...His heart loves you!**

# Who Was I Supposed to Be?

Mother, who was I supposed to be?

What plans did you have for me?

Did you want me to be as **sweet and loving** as you?

Or, did you want me to find my own way through?

Mother, why were we separated so soon?

I didn't even get to see one morn or noon?

Did you know Mother I felt your fears?

Was it for me your eyes filled with tears?


Oh Mother, I so much wanted to be your comfort and joy,

To be your munchkin, your sweetie-pie, your living toy!

Coming home from work, traversing all those miles,

I so much wanted to give you cute little social
smiles.

Methinks **more than all**, I was yearning for your
pure sweet love,

While I reposed on your breasts, peaceful like a
snow-white dove.

But it wasn't to be...instead; I am the source of your
sorrow,

The pain that pierces your womb leaving it tender
and hollow.

I left you hopeless, comfortless, and God forbid,
almost lifeless,

Your memory of me only makes you sad, gloomy,
and speechless.

Horror grasped thy soul and a dark cloud hovered
over thee,

Rivers of tears flowed, when you realized, you were
losing me.

I could not forgive myself for bruising your inner
feeling,

So, I was determined to find **Someone** to bring you
healing.

As I transcended this "life" I couldn't help but feel
that I was to see its Essence,

So awesome in power, yet so deep in love, I could
entrust myself to His Presence.

I saw His Shepherd-like figure surrounded by
children flying in the skies,

As I gazed at Him, He smiled at me and **wiped the
tears from my eyes.**

With eyes of love, He told me, **to tell you** "Be still,
and know that **I AM GOD...**

I am with you my lowly, grieving daughter,
wherever on earth you may trod."

See, though I am safe with Him here, He is right by
your side...

I doubt not that in His deep, deep love you can
forever abide.

The Sovereign Lord separated us "temporarily", so
that I can live in a better place,

Oh Mom, I am filled with unspeakable joy, for only
here can I see Him face-to-face.

Mom, accept the Sovereign Lord's decision to
transport me to heaven,

Where one day, I am absolutely sure, **we will see
each other again.**

# Treasured Memories of Mom

Happy Mother's Day milady with much love
So soon flown away like a peaceful dove
Loving you more than these stanzas explain
Mom, in my heart you shall forever remain

Life so short, you're gone eternally
But your love is kept alive mentally
Sweet words flowed from your poetry
Parker fountain pen oozed ingenuity

My classy mother, petite to perfection
So full of warmth, agape and affection
Ever lovely, bubbly, spunky and witty
Caught the eye of the one & only "Smitty"!

Reminiscing on nights you stayed in my bed
With your gentle hand, caressing my head
Making melody in my ears, as I got wheezier:
"Ooh-oo Child! Things are gonna get easier"!

Came your malady, my turn to "sing" at night:
"Here comes the sun...And I say...It's all right."
You personified the optimism of the cantata
I love and miss you, "little darling" Nina!

# Take It Easy and Go Through

**(Tribute to Dad)**

"Tek it easy an' go tru," advises dad as he ends
conversation
To lift engine from Toyota, Gary puts pulley into
position
While the tall, handsome, grey-haired man of wit &
wisdom
Rakes leaves under the mango & cherry trees they
fell from
Then starts the overhaul, while grass is moistened
with dew
With torque wrench in hand, Daddy now starts to
unscrew
"The kids" were raised by strong hands oft-times
greasy:
The beautifully intelligent Suzan, Ayon, Julian &
Stacy


"The kids" were his love, his life, his pride, his prize
When he speaks of us, affection lights his hazel eyes
The dearly loved neighbourhood mechanic also liked
cricket
Dad was listening and cheering as the Windies took
a wicket
The pigeons converge as I throw some corn on the
ground

Ayon feeds the frisky rabbits, as guinea pigs
scamper around
Julian picks some Ackees, so lunch will have a nice
mouthfeel
Billy kneads the flour to boil dumplings nicknamed
"cartwheel"

Late in the afternoon, Glen pulls up in his silver-grey
Escort
Before greeting Glen, Basil washes his hands by the
carport
The Ford needed bodywork and Dad was adept at
spraying lacquer
As they talked, Ben walked to his dark blue Fiat with
a spanner
After deciding on Duco colour, Dad goes inside to
prepare dinner
Jean-Pierre helps but the aroma from food makes
him a grinner
As Dad adds Grace broad beans to the cowfoot in
the kitchen
He remembers that Ayon wants to eat only chicken
Whether he's frying fish, pot-roasting beef, or
currying goat
For Ayon's sake, he just adds the chicken to the
same "boat"

At eventide, his dear friend Larry drinks with his
"rumpanions"
He and Dad challenge Maxi & Gary, vying for
"domino champions"
Suzan and Stacy sit on the patio with friends in loud
chatter

Music from Dad's speakers yields to their high-
pitched laughter
So, the unassuming mechanic was not made with
auto-metal
Truly our hero, he was made with a tender-heart of
love eternal
A tenderness evident in many of his soulfully classic
song choices
More so, in his affection for "the kids", the reason
Daddy rejoices

# Sweet Sister Sarita

Sweet Sister Sarita...
Still miss you after all these years
Down my cheeks still roll the tears
So sad to know you already left us
An adorable girl, a cute little genius
Love you sister, so special to my heart
Endlessly energetic and incredibly smart
Doing the best that a young mother can
Loving your boys, Jhevanté and Nathan

Sweet Sister Sarita...
Your potential had wild blue yonder as limit
But double-distress so young broke your spirit
Within two years, experienced two grievous losses
Followed by sleepless nights of turns and tosses
Your dad's passing summoned sorrowful shake
Then losing mom was like an emotional quake
Unbearable, everything inside you churned
Oft expressed how much your heart burned

Sweet Sister Sarita...
An aspiring lawyer, you were the legal kind
But orphaned so early, impacted your mind
You sometimes wished you too could have died
Gave up mentally, though tearfully we tried...
Entreated you but at times you stared in space
Seemed you were travelling to another place
No longer that endearing, cheery child
We lost lovely lady in a melancholic wild

Sweet Sister Sarita...
The family had another sorrow to witness
Mercilessly lost your struggle with sickness
A painful loss of one so beautifully nice
From my heart felt like one took a slice
Your untimely departure we cannot atone
But we are so thankful for the brief "loan"
Live on sweet "Princess", as your name implies,
In celestial castle where your memory never dies!

# Keep Walking

## (Tribute to co-worker Peta-Gaye)

During that last 5K Walk, we did the first four
kilometres, but the race wasn't finished...

so we kept walking...

We finished the race and had breakfast, but we had
to go back to our separate lives...

so we kept walking...

Two weeks later, I got a very disturbing call that she
was sick and had to be hospitalized, but I felt sure
that

she would...keep walking...

Our hearts were ripped to pieces and everything
seemed to crash all around us when we learned that
this bright spark of light had transitioned to another
life ...even then, we denied it and kept saying...

she was still walking...

But even as Peta went through the different phases
of the walk, we too must go through different
phases of grief and laughter; sorrow and joy; failure
and success; darker and brighter; bitter and better...

and just keep walking...

Even after losing my mom at age 45, my dad at age 53 and my little sister at age 21...I had no choice, but to...

keep walking...

They left us saying, "we wish...we wish...we wish..." We keep asking: why, why, why?  Why so soon? Why leave us in agony over losing you...but we have to, we must...

keep walking...

Knowing full well that they will never again be seen in this life, and that no one will ever take their places in our hearts...with tears rolling and heart grieving...we must...

keep walking...

We will not survive the bitter throes of a massive loss by becoming frozen...or the unexpected challenges of life by being inactive...we will make it through all these things, if we just...

keep walking...

And so family and friends, reflect on the precious memories she left us, think on the principles she wanted us to live by, light your way with her loving smile...

just keep walking...and make her proud!

# Dear Mother

## (Tribute to Aunt Ritty)

Dear mother, last night we dreamed of you, looking
regal and at rest
We saw you in heaven, in pearly white, you so
beautifully dressed,
When you saw us, your eyes lit up and you smiled
brightly
You walked up and embraced us, oh,
so tightly,
Tears rolled from our eyes when you looked at us
You said, *"Don't cry! I'm finally home and it's
joyous"*
*"My strength was gone, but my love for you was
strong*
*I saw angels coming for me, in a majestic throng*
*But I didn't want to miss the opportunity to see you
all*
*So I prayed for a few more days and they heard my
call*
*Instead of taking me to heaven, they accompanied
me to Florida*
***Mi glad bag buss*** *when I saw the family, I felt like
I was in euphoria*
*One angel pointed to his clock, but I pleaded, 'Not
while they're here'*
*So, after you all left, he spirited me away to the
heavenly sphere"*

But Miss Ritts, your timing was so peculiar, it's like you planned it,
We thought you'd be at Aunt Phyl's party, but you didn't make it.
*"But I was there," you declared.  "Didn't Phyllis tell you?"*
*That's the one time she kept a secret from you!*
*And Oh, I was dancing off **mi old foot dem***
***"She's Royal"** is **my** song, even in heavenly realm*
*Weep not my children, you are my royal treasure*
*Over the years, I derived from you so much pleasure"*


We miss you dearly mother, we so love and we so appreciate you
It wasn't just for 9 months, but all our lives you carried us through
We can't thank you enough, our gratitude for your life runs deep
Even when our tears dry, our hearts will still weep
*"I see your agony," you sweetly whispered. "But I'm in a better place"*
*I'm out of my suffering, and I'm in absolute peace*
*I know you feel like you can't make it without me,*
*I see you broken in tears, and deep in agony*
*But I'm always with you, as your loving mother I did my part*
*Though I'm gone in body, my love always remains in your heart!"*

Keep sweet, dear mother, one day we'll reunite,
Mother of mothers, you put up a good fight
The world may have lost a spark so bright
But the heavens have gained a glorious light!

# Mother's Love

## (Tribute to Aunt Mag)

Mother's love is unceasing,
As her entire life had shown.
Her love was much stronger
Than the pain that took her home.
My heart is now heavy with sorrow,
My face all stained with tears.
Tears bespeak how much I miss her,
But never shall I forget her years.
Oh, my heart is a river of emotions:
Overflowing with sorrow...
Mixed with waves of love...
Flooding my bones and marrow.

Her memories linger: I hear her voice,
*I can see her sweetly, smiling face.*
And though my heart is heavy,
It holds her in a **very** special place!

Mother's love is unfailing,
Like a rock she's underneath me.
She holds me up day by day,
Filling my life with energy.
It's wlth a grateful heart I say,
I love my mother endlessly.
She's left a void deep within me,
For this is a heart-rending finality.
O gentle soul with a love so pure,
Alas! thou hast forever gone from me.

But the heavens rejoice to see,
A spirit as sweet as thee!
A mother of exemplary strength,
Has found rest in eternity!

Mother's love is unchanging,
So it's not for me to live in despair.
It's for me to be proud of who I am,
For I am the result of your tender care.
I watched you graciously handle success,
And how you persevered through difficulty.
Neither of these changed your love,
You remained my source of stability.
I cried when I saw you ailing,
I would've done anything to bear your pain!
As your body failed before my eyes,
My soul was torn to pieces!
But love overcomes all boundaries,
For your love outlives your suffering.

So mom, all that I can do,
Is make a solemn promise to you:
To always portray to the world the best of me,
For your undying love, lives on in me!

# My Solace & Strength in My Sorrow

Deep in sorrow is my heart plunged,
As the love of my life no longer breathes.
After so many years of loving friendship,
A chasm between life and death is created.
In the home, filled with well-wishers,
A lonesome sorrow overwhelmed my soul.
There was "organized chaos" concerning:
Programmes, flowers, songs, pictures...
So many people to hug,
So many faces to greet,
So many words to hear,
But none could assuage the pain of
My sorrow!

Suddenly, my eyes caught yours...
As you arrived, peace engulfed my being.
Sorrow & joy blended perfectly in my soul:
Sorrow, because I lost the love of my life,
Joy, because you magically appeared.
O the warmth of your embrace!
In a tender moment when time froze,
My numb spirit revived and felt warm.
Now I feel that I can face tomorrow's burial.
Your strong love permeated my heart.

A moment of solace drowned out the chaos!
Because of the special bond we share,
I was comfortable being vulnerable with you.
My solace!

At dawn, I awoke to a picturesque sunrise.
The blooming ginger lilies said, "Good morning!"
With the love of my life, now lifeless,
I was weak;
But your strong hand guided me to the chapel,
Where you stood by me like a guardian angel!
In my feebleness, you were my tower of strength!
Some brought flowers, many sent cards,
While others contributed in other ways.
But in my time of deepest sorrow,
All I needed was your hand to hold,
I just wanted your chest, upon which to rest.
During the service and at the burial,
Even as the tears flowed, you held me close.
I made it through the day because of you:
Because of your comforting presence,
Your display of graceful strength.
That's all I needed to take me through...
Short was your visit, but every moment cherished.
You've gone, but I feel the embrace of
Your love that will not let go...
My strength!

# Words 'R' Us

## (Tribute to Uncle Sheldon)

A thesaurus in human edition, emitting legalese with
conviction
Prior to any discussion, ensure you have mental
version
How do we thee herald? Wordsmith or
Wordmcdonald?
Eloquent with vast vocabulary, breathing words like
a dictionary
Distinction in education, dissertation on negotiation
Your style was rudimentary, but result was
documentary
A master of argument, oppose at your detriment!

School was your locus, excellence was your focus
Though the path was tedious, your work was sheer
genius
Insatiable appetite for education, excelled after
every matriculation
Legal knowledge was encyclopaedic, your
scholarship was eclectic
A Maritime Areas buff, grasped its issues like a cuff
Thou brilliant law icon, I dub thee "Legal Don"!

Forever grateful for your life, but your death cuts
like a knife
I will miss the fun times, so dedicate to you a few
rhymes
You were our "Lord Protector", mess with us but
turn defector
A beneficiary of your care, for me you were always
there
One theme on my mind, life touched by friend so
kind
Cared not for fortune and fame, but told us to use
your name!

Working hand in glove, keeping us bonded in love
Impacted by your sacrifice, but your presence would
suffice
I can't pay you back, for the kindness you stack
Tie absent from your wardrobe, but uncle travelled
the globe
Not a man of fanciful fashion, but one full of decisive
action
Won't forget the meal-budgeting, mouth with burger
bulging!

Lost you in tragic accident, brought us closer but
despondent
Your last days were painful, the whole family was
tearful
Too soon losing some of you, can't have a family of
few
Mom, dad & sis died young, now you...by death
stung
No longer among contemporaries, we cherish sweet
memories

We are eternally thankful; we are emotionally
"loveful"
We express love and honour, to a gentleman and
scholar
Our hearts perpetually salute, a man whose life bore
much fruit!

# SPECIAL OCCASION

# Music is Dennis Alcapone's Life

**(Celebrating Uncle Dennis' 70th Birthday)**

"From the Number One Station, here comes the Power
Version"
The hottest MC in radio land, spewing lyrics with a
musical band
Voice insured for over a million, commands the stage like
a stallion
"The king of the record track", making melodious hits
back-to-back

Across the Pond flew Uncle D, landed on Jamrock during
ChikV
Before the first night he spent, protected himself with
repellent
As he sped-off in a red Mustang, he grinned his gold
teeth and sang:
"Mosquito one, mosquito two, mosquito jump inna hot
callaloo" (Kill dat!)

When Dennis met cute Elaine, he sang to her thru
window pane:
"A dis ya a fiya, a dis ya a suga", "Love I for-eva...love I
for-eva"
Off they went into the Moonlight, then Elaine glowed so
bright:
"And that's why you're my lover, YESSSS...you are MYYY
lover."

For him she'll go the extra mile, in London they live in
"Fine Style"
"Stick by me, I'll stick by you", never make you lose, this
I promise to do
"Can't you see, we were meant to be? Like the birds in
the tree"
So you see why 'Laine love I, 'cause I'm a different kinda
guy


His priority has always been, that we "Teach the
Children":
"R-A-T rat, M-A-T mat, C-A-T cat, Look at dat, look at
dat"
He links love with being happy, Love makes your heart
sappy
Be happy with love-power, keeps you fresh like a nice
shower


So, World leave 'Pone alone..., 'cause he's a Big Man in
this town!
"Keep on rocking, keep on moving, Keep on skanking,
keep on grooving"
You gave me insights as a lanky lad, unique perspectives
on my loving dad
For that I'm forever indebted to thee, my ebullient,
effervescent Uncle D!

# *Like A....*

**(Celebrating Aunt Ritty's 80th Birthday)**

*Like a stallion…*
*…strong, determined, firm…*
*…Ms Rick forged her way from Chapelton*
            *to her Long Island pavilion*


*Like a freight train…*
*…powerful, forceful, dutiful…*
*…Aunt Ritty carried her family across hard terrain*
            *so, now she can easily refrain*


*Like a flower…*
*…brilliant, elegant, resplendent…*
*…Retinella delicately and beautifully blossomed*
*each hour*
            *…brightening the world with her power*


*Like an Easter bun…*
*…sweet spot, weak spot, tender spot…*
*…when Ionie bake 'ar toto, cake, gizzada, bun*
            *all oder bakers get up and run*


*Like a mother…*
*…emotionally connected, open-minded, tender-*
*hearted…*

*…yes, tender at times, rough at times, but caring at*
**<u>all</u>** *times*
*…Aunt Ritty is a one-of-kind, rare gem…precious &*
*priceless*
*…mother, GRAND-mother, GREAT-grandmother,*
*aunt, sister, cousin, friend…*
*…Moma is the BESTEST*
*…Mom is my boonoonoonoos*
*…Ms Rick you're the most FAVOURITESTED!*

*So, be EMBIGGENED!*

# My Other Mother
# (M.O.M.)

(Celebrating Aunt Phyl's 80th Birthday)

Each year, time is made to laud people on
special days
For you, I can take every day to sing your
praise
You're one of the most loving persons I've ever
known
Your kindness to me, in word and deed you've
shown
The impact you've made on my life is without
measure
You are among the family's precious treasure
As you're looking so beautiful on your
birthday
This is indeed, a very special
day!

It's wonderful to find a treasure in someone who
has precious advice
But better to find a person who backs that with
tremendous sacrifice
What my parents could not afford to
do
Your faithful support helped me to make it
through

Do you know why we never worry about your
shape?
That's because you're Superwoman without a
cape!


You're a wonder-woman, in whose arms I found
comfort for countless hours
With the passing of Mom & Dad, two of earth's
gone-too-soon flowers
The challenges of those unexpected deaths left
me on the verge of despair
But I'm forever grateful that this stalwart, met
me there.
Through your careful counsel, my life grew
better as the months grew old,
With your sweet spirit, the light got brighter as
the years unfold
You talked me through the days, weeks, months
and the years
You walked me through the struggle, strife,
sorrow, and the fears


I will forever cherish you because years ago
when in a very dark hour
You shone the light of the kindest words from
your tower
That you could say, "You were the son I never
had" was remarkable
In my weakest moment, the boost it gave me
was incalculable
No difficult situation did you ever shun

You lifted me and proved to me that I was a son
Even though I sometimes disappointed you
Your love for me was genuine, deep, and true

So, even though I made fun of the size of your
bra!
In a sense, it houses the part of you from which
I can draw
For, so large is your heart, it keeps the entire
family enshrined
This just goes to show that you're awesome,
meek and kind
For that, you'll always hold a special place in my
heart
Since I've proven that nothing can keep us
apart!

If the planet should ever host a Family World
Cup
There would be one home from which I would
sup
If we were to select the captain for our World
Cup team
We'd pick someone with tenacity to fulfil our
winning dream
She's easily the most audacious person we
know
For she's marshalled us so that we successfully
grow
She's a skilful captain who's a family
foundation

A unique player we're fortunate to have in our
generation
So, as we celebrate your special day
It's my distinct honour and great pleasure to
say:
The trophy for **"My Other Mother",** a woman
of awesome skill
Is presented to this ebullient, elegant woman of
the strongest will.

# Baby Shower

We have gathered today for your baby shower,
For you have within your garden a little, tender
flower.
This flower started from the planting of a seed,
In fertile ground where only your mister can
feed!
The seed travelled within a rich fluid,
Spewed from a nozzle as a thick liquid


If baby is anything like its mother,
We know challenge will not be a bother.
For we always see you in your splendour and
beauty,
Taking on difficulty with a great sense of duty.
Each day, as she does her utmost to meet a
deadline
She feels a jolt, but keeps on working, holding
her spine!


If baby's thoughts could be displayed on the
ultra-sound screen
You would see the words of baby: "Mom, this is
what I mean:
I would love to tell a story about my beautiful
mother,
She is so gracefully professional...like no other.

I love you mother with all my heart and soul,
Please know that your protection is my goal.
The other day at work when you felt me turning
and kicking,
Hush!  It wasn't intended for you, as you were
just there ticking.
When the transaction failed and brought the
system to a halt,
Someone made funny-face at you as if it was
your fault.
"Watch over my mommy," I asked the Maker up
above,
And He replied, "Yes, I will....with *eyes of tender
love.*"

# *Farewell*

You're leaving us today, but we laud you as a special one,

For through integrity, every challenge you've won.

You are special, wonderful, and one-of-a-kind,

Your approach to life shows you have a beautiful mind.

You're a rare combination of beauty and brains,

And behind your sweet looks, no nonsense obtains!

You are gifted, talented, very intellectual,

And in your assigned tasks, you were highly effectual.

Your level of professionalism has left us very impressed,

You have completed your mission without being distressed.

You carried out your work with such gusto and zest,

We had to conclude that you were "simply the best"!

As you go on your odyssey fulfil your dreams,

Remember that life sometimes has tempestuous streams.

The tenacious spirit under your captivating smile,

Will make you achieve anything in your elegant style!

We wish you grand success in your life's aim,

Keep dreaming till one day you become that great dame!

# *Graduation*

Honoured People, before we, this grand ceremony
Cease;
Methinks that this great school developed a
Masterpiece.

We bid farewell because opportunities abound out
There;
With mentors at your side, you have nothing to
Fear.

Perhaps you felt like the course material weighed a
Mega-Ton;
But in your quest for learning, I hope you carried a
Ton-a-Fun.

To all you studious graduates, I wish your training to
Manifest,
Into something that proves you are absolutely the
Best.

As you go on your odyssey with new-found
Skill;
Combine this education, with a tenacious
Will.

So that the knowledge imbibed, not come to
Nought;
May I bequeath you with one final, provoking
Thought:

View not nagging issues, as status quo for which to
Settle;
Rather, treat them as "good problems", to show
your true
Mettle.

May your careers be fraught with challenges
resembling
Midnight,
So that, to your managers, you may display a
brilliant
Sunlight!

# Like Fine Wine

## (Retirement)

Like grapes churning in a winepress,
You endured target-making stress.
Thus releasing your creative juices,
That only the best grape produces.
Fermented into an exotic brand,
Placed on a fancy display stand.
Enjoyed by the connoisseur;
The delight of the consumer.


With colleagues, we spend cherished time,
Like a collection of exquisite wine.
In various stages of our careers,
Our hearts and minds develop in the cellars,
Ere poured into glasses to achieve targets,
Or stored longer for special projects.


We see the many years swiftly pass,
As you work with finesse and class.
And here we are again, back at the winery
Where you transformed, your "refinery"!
We popped a bottle, your career to celebrate,
Surprised, we asked "Did you change the grape?"
"No," said the vintner, "It's the same!"
"But it's more delicious!" we exclaim.
Serving the company with distinction,
Like fine wine, you've aged to perfection!

Like fine wine, you've developed over the ages,
With deeper wisdom, you've become graceful sages.
For your many years of excellent service,
Our gratitude to you is sincerest!
We applaud your unwavering dedication,
We love you for your fiery passion.
We wish for you in this sentiment,
A very gratifying retirement!
To your finest years,
We raise a toast and say, Cheers!

TRIBUTE TO
ESSENTIAL
WORKERS

# Service With Heart

Across the globe, in every store
We see physically distant shoppers galore
Working in the stores is a very special bunch
Selling everything from sanitizer to fruit punch

This dedicated team you just can't beat
Serving tirelessly on nimble feet
Customers get a great feeling in this place
You can experience it by the smile on each face.

There was an old lady who spoke with eyes popped
Yes, she boasted till her dentures almost dropped,
"This is my favourite place to shop,
Because the service, none can top!"

Oh, and there was a toddler in a loaded trolley;
She spoke sweetly whilst clutching her pretty dolly.
"Oh mommy, I'm in food-heaven…I feel so jolly.
Leave the rice, so I can come back with Aunt Polly!"

You are a beacon in every part
You are an excellent food mart
Covid is here and you are even busier
Making our lives so much easier.

From curb side to home delivery, and online
This team goes the extra mile every time.
With the best service and your smile
We feel safe in every aisle.
And those frequent savings
Make us give-in to our many cravings!

# Sticktoitivity

Together we're Team Agility
Building a world class company
Nothing's too hard for this family
'Cause we possess "sticktoitivity"

We stick to it
We stick to it
We stick to it
And we never quit!

We are here thankful to be alive
To beat this virus, we must all strive
Our success is what fate inscribes
Because this team is full of vibes...

We stick to it
We stick to it
We stick to it
And we never quit!

We're fighting the virus everyday
Then come new variants to hold sway
Approved vaccines are on their way
Shot in arms so we can be okay

We stick to it
We stick to it
We stick to it
And we never quit!

# The Crucible of Coronavirus

Working from home is far more efficient
As I'm just a few steps from the kitchen.
There, I learned to make a pancake batter
Instead of being at work to harbour chatter.
We converted a bedroom to an office;
The living room became a class;
But LIVE sports resumed, so tv den was unchanged;
As I watched teams win championships!
At times, home felt the movies as my daughter
Flew around like Wonder Woman in theatre!

To make the targets, I'm busting my chops;
Working day and night, by many coffee cups.
Zooming for hours can be enormously taxing,
But breeze through coconut tree is relaxing.
So, in these dangerous, "covidious" times
To maintain my sanity, I write some rhymes
Grocery shopping was my social odyssey,
But man I had to switch to "click & delivery".
The coronavirus took a lasting toll,
While we grieve for lives this virus stole
Unable to see loved ones for months on end,
From afar, we support in sickness and death.
In the crucible of coronavirus
We remain positively "vibrous"!

# You're the "Specialest"!

Essential workers are awesome:
You come in early
You work so late
You do great things
You do the little things
Most people don't see
But you don't complain
Just stick to your game!
You work with finesse
You're the finest!

Essential workers are intelligent:
Think on your feet
Don't skip a beat
Work with a smile
Go the extra mile
You keep us on track
You keep us in check
Give your all every day
With no time to play
You're the smartest!

Essential workers are special:
Your effort is blest
Your work is the best
You are so patient
You are so kind
In all that you do
In all that you say
With care and grace

You light up the place
You're the brightest!

Essential workers are special:
We applaud you because
You're astoundingly awesome
We appreciate you because
You're amazingly adorable
We admire you because
You're awesomely delightful
We acclaim you because
You're wondrously elegant
We commend you because
You're courteously charming
We respect you because
You're adoringly resplendent
We honour you today
We honour you **every day**
Because you're the "specialest"!

# About the Author

Wayne A. C. Smith lives in Jamaica. Known as a Master of Ceremonies, Wayne writes poetry for events such as weddings, funerals, birthdays, baby showers, retirement functions and goodbyes. This is Wayne's first published work. His work embodies personal experiences of life, death and love. Wayne holds a B.Sc. (Hons.) in Chemical Engineering from The University of the West Indies. In 2011, he completed his MBA at the Mona School of Business & Management and graduated with **Distinction** in Banking and Finance. He received a certificate of achievement for "Outstanding Performance" in the Banking & Finance Concentration.

Wayne enjoys swimming, playing table tennis, and writing comedy & poetry.

Contact Wayne via
E-mail: wacsmith2001@yahoo.com
Twitter: @WayneACSmith